DOLLARS
& SENSE

Bible Wisdom
for the
Faithful Steward

LARRY BURKETT

Edited by Adeline Griffith

BARBOUR
PUBLISHING, INC.
Uhrichsville, Ohio

DOLLARS & SENSE

*Bible Wisdom
for the
Faithful Steward*

ACKNOWLEDGMENTS

This book could not have been prepared for release without the gracious permission received from the following publishers:

Moody Press, Chicago, IL

Thomas Nelson Publishers, Nashville, TN

Victor Books, Wheaton, IL

The Lockman Foundation

The International Bible Society

Tyndale House Publishers

Excluding Scripture passages, all material in this book was excerpted from the following books by Larry Burkett:

Business by the Book (Thomas Nelson Publishers), *The Coming Economic Earthquake* (Moody Press), *The Complete Financial Guide for Couples* (Victor Books), *The Complete Financial Guide for Single Parents* (Victor Books), *Debt-Free Living* (Moody Press), *Financial Freedom Library* (Volume I and II) (Moody Press), *Investing for the Future* (Victor Press), *Preparing for Retirement* (Moody Press), *Using Your Money Wisely* (Moody Press), *What the Bible Says About Money* (Moody Press), *Your Finances in Changing Times* (Moody Press)

Scripture verses marked TLB: Taken from The Living Bible, © 1971. Used by permission of Tyndale House Publishers, Inc. All rights reserved.

Scripture verses marked NAS: Taken from the New American Standard Bible, © 1960, 1962, 1963, 1968, 1971, 1972, 1973, 1975, 1977 by the Lockman Foundation. Used by Permission.

Scripture verses marked NIV: Taken from the Holy Bible, New International Version. ® © 1973, 1978, 1984 by International Bible Society. All rights reserved. Used by Permission.

Published by   Barbour Publishing, Inc.
                 P.O. Box 719
                 Uhrichsville, Ohio 44683
                 http://www.barbourbooks.com

Printed in the United States of America.

ABUNDANCE

*"Your abundance being
a supply for their want,
that their abundance also may
become a supply for your want,
that there may be equality"*
(2 Corinthians 8:14 NAS).

*T*he majority of warnings in Christ's messages were to the wealthy, not the poor. Just having an abundance is not a sign of God's blessings. A disciplined lifestyle with an abundance is greater witness than the abundance could ever be.

ACCOUNTABILITY

*"Why do you call Me,
'Lord, Lord,'
and do not do what I say?"*
(Luke 6:46 NAS)

*P*erhaps nothing is needed more than accountability. Many Christians are violating basic biblical principles in the areas of personal and business finances. God is under no obligation to bail them out of situations He has specifically warned them against in the first place. That doesn't mean He won't. If Christ is the total and absolute authority in our lives, we will obey His teachings.

ACCUMULATION

*"Whoever wishes to become
great among you shall be your
servant, and whoever wishes
to be first among you shall be
your slave; just as the Son
of Man did not come to be
served, but to serve"*
(Matthew 20:26-28 NAS).

*A*ll that truly matters is what we can do for the kingdom of God. The things we accumulate are not important; they are only tools for us to use in accomplishing God's work. God owns it all anyway. The accumulation of money is a major deterrent to a humble spirit. The tendency is to desire to be served rather than to serve.

ADVERSITY

*I*n God's discipleship plan some adversity is necessary for spiritual maturity. Life is a mixture of good times and bad, and we don't know what the future will bring. Although things might not be going well, God wants us to trust Him. God may use your adversities as a testimony for other people or to reinforce a lesson.

"Many are the afflictions of the righteous; but the Lord delivers him out of them all" (Psalm 34:19 NAS).

ANXIETY

*A*nxiety is produced over financial responsibility; and the family's basic needs are not met because of past or present buying practices. Don't seek escape during difficulties; seek peace during them.

"Be anxious for nothing, but in everything by prayer and supplication with thanksgiving let your requests be made known to God" (Philippians 4:6 NAS).

ATTITUDE

*A*bove all else, God is concerned with our attitudes. God wants to bless and prosper His people according to His plan for their lives. The key to God's provision is attitude—the attitude of being a steward, or manager, and not an owner.

"Who then is the faithful and sensible steward, whom his master will put in charge of his servants, to give them their rations at the proper time?" (Luke 12:42 NAS)

AUTHORITY, FINANCIAL

*A*nyone in authority must exercise great caution to maintain the proper balance. Authority actually means responsibility according to God's Word. God's plan for authority is not an either/or situation. It is a joint effort with differing responsibilities.

AUTHORITY, GOD'S

*S*ince problems are day-by-day occurrences, our acknowledgment of God's authority and forgiveness should be daily as well. Authority is not conditional; nor is earthly authority absolute. You don't have to look very far into God's Word to see that authority is God's system of keeping order in a fallen society.

AUTOMOBILES

*I*n our mobile society an automobile is no longer a luxury. Except in large metropolitan areas where public transportation is available, it is a necessity. The cost of maintaining and operating a car is enormous and can be a budget-buster. No matter what happens to your old car, it is almost always cheaper to repair the one you own than to purchase a new one.

AVOIDING DISASTER

I've never counseled a couple who said, "Our five-year goal was to get miserably into debt, hate each other, stop praying and attending church, and now we're right where we want to be." Yet, that's where a lot of couples are. The way to avoid such a disaster is to never let it happen in the first place.

"With all my heart I want your blessings. Be merciful just as you promised. I thought about the wrong direction in which I was headed, and turned around and came running back to you" (Palsm 119:58-60 TLB).

AVOIDING REALITY

*O*ne way to relieve tension temporarily is to pretend that no problem exists. Business owners have been known to manipulate every conceivable angle in an attempt to prolong the life of a hopeless business even one more day, waiting for a miracle to reverse the situation. I believe in miracles, but I have observed that God doesn't violate His scriptural principles to accomplish His goals; He always follows His own rules.

"Praise be to you, O LORD. . . I meditate on your precepts and consider your ways. I delight in your decrees; I will not neglect your word" (Palsm 119:12,15-16 NIV).

11

BANKRUPTCY

*B*ankruptcy is a serious matter and, at best, both sides lose. The creditors lose much of the money they are owed, and the debtors lose much of the respect they previously had. A person who has filed for bankruptcy can turn a negative situation into a positive one by making a commitment to repay what is legitimately owed. God's Word clearly says that a believer should be responsible for his or her promises and repay what is owed.

"Don't withhold repayment of your debts. Don't say 'some other time,' if you can pay now" (Proverbs 3:27-28 TLB).

BENEVOLENCE

*T*he Bible teaches that we should help fellow Christians in need and also show hospitality to strangers. Thus, every member of any local church should be able to look to the fellowship they attend as an extension of God's provision.

"If you have a friend who is in need of food and clothing, and you say to him, 'Well, good-bye and God bless you; stay warm and eat hearty,' and then don't give him clothes or food, what good does that do?" (James 2:15-16 TLB)

BONDAGE

*B*eing in financial bondage means having excessive debts, which usually occurs because of bad habits. Many years ago financial bondage meant physical bondage; failure to pay a debt was equated with dishonesty, which was judged strictly. Today society usually doesn't incarcerate someone because of debts; literal physical bondage has been replaced by mental bondage.

"Come to terms quickly with your enemy before it is too late and he drags you into court and you are thrown into a debtor's cell, for you will stay there until you have paid the last penny" (Matthew 5:25-26 TLB).

BORROWING

*C*hristians who are trapped by borrowing have violated one or more of the scriptural principles God has given. He says that when someone borrows, he or she becomes a servant of the lender; the lender becomes an authority over the borrower. This clearly defines God's attitude about borrowing.

"The rich rules over the poor, and the borrower becomes the lender's slave" (Proverbs 22:7).

BREATHING, FINANCIAL

*N*eed a plan for financial breathing? God's plan is simple. It is exhaling bad habits and inhaling good principles. It is the Holy Spirit that simplifies this plan for us if we allow Him to.

"Come and have mercy on me as is your way with those who love you. Lord, listen to my prayers; give me the common sense you promised. Hear my prayers; rescue me as you said you would" (Psalm 119:132,169-170 TLB).

BRIBERY

*B*ribery can come in the form of flattering words, inappropriate gifts—even raises and promotions. Maintain integrity at all costs.

"The wise man is turned into a fool by a bribe; it destroys his understanding. Bribes blind the eyes of the wisest and corrupt their decisions" (Ecclesiastes 7:7, Deuteronomy 16:19 TLB).

BROKENNESS

*B*rokenness, whether financial, physical, emotional, or all three, has at its center the purpose of teaching us to trust in God. He is in control. If we are serving Him, nothing can befall us unless He allows it.

"And we know that God causes all things to work together for good to those who love God, to those who are called according to His purpose" (Romans 8:28 NAS).

BUDGETING

A budget is no more than a plan to balance spending with income. It controls spending and will help in developing a surplus. A budget is not magical; it will not work by itself; you must put it into practice. It should be a reflection of you and a plan to bring peace, not conflict, into your home.

"Commit to the Lord whatever you do, and your plans will succeed" (Proverbs 16:3 NIV).

BUSINESS

*T*he purpose of any Christian in business is to glorify God, not just to make a profit. One key to being faithful to the Lord is making decisions on the basis of God's Word and not on circumstances, feelings, or what is acceptable to society.

"Commit your works to the Lord, And your plans will be established. The Lord has made everything for its own purpose" (Proverbs 16:3-4 NAS).

BUSINESS TITHING

*B*usiness tithing is not dramatically different from personal tithing. However, figuring a business tithe is not necessarily as clear-cut as figuring your personal tithe. You should tithe on business increase, which may not be the same as the gross, because you are dealing with noncash assets as well as stocks. Only in prayer can you decide how best to honor the Lord through your business.

"A tithe of everything from the land [business], whether grain from the soil or fruit from the trees, belongs to the Lord; it is holy to the Lord" (Leviticus 27:30 NIV).

BUYING

A common misconception is that the majority of spending in a marriage is done by the wife. Not so. Men don't buy often, but when they do they buy big-ticket items. There are some simple rules for you to follow before buying anything. First, don't buy anything unless you wait at least thirty days. Second, get at least three different prices on that item. Third, never have more than one item on your "want" list at one time.

"We have brought nothing into the world, so we cannot take anything out of it either. If we have food and covering, with these we shall be content" (1 Timothy 6:7-8 NAS).

CHEATING

Many times Christians tell about how other Christians willfully cheated them and several others out of their money. The Scriptures admonish anyone who cheats in any way.

CHECKBOOKS

It's impossible to have your finances under control without understanding the basics of good bookkeeping. A large percentage of young couples don't know how to balance a checkbook and have no idea of how much they are spending.

*"There is a way which
seems right to a man,
but its end is
the way of death"*
(Proverbs 14:12 NAS).

CHILD CARE

The cost of child care won't compute in the average family budget; and it certainly won't compute in a single parent's more limited budget. Unfortunately, the churches have not taken the lead in helping to solve the dilemma.

*"If, as my representatives,
you give even a cup of cold
water to a little child,
you will surely be rewarded"*
(Matthew 10:42 TLB).

CHILD SUPPORT

*C*hildren have no choice in their circumstances. They didn't choose to be born to us. They were given into our care by God. A parent cannot refuse his or her responsibility to the children under any circumstances.

"If anyone does not provide for his relatives, and especially for his immediate family, he has denied the faith and is worse than an unbeliever" (1 Timothy 5:8 NIV).

CHILDREN

*T*each your children that God owns everything by allowing them to see this principle in your life. Pray about your material needs and let God provide them without borrowing so your children can see God is real. Raise your children the way you should have been raised.

"Teach a child to choose the right path, and when he is older he will remain upon it" (Proverbs 22:6 TLB).

CHILDREN'S DISCIPLINE

*P*arents cannot establish financial discipline in their children if they themselves are undisciplined. Teach your children that everyone needs to live on a budget. Children who have been taught the basic principles of money management early and have proved their ability to use them wisely could be trusted to handle a credit card with no problem.

"A wise son brings joy to his father, but a foolish man despises his mother" (Proverbs 15:20 NIV).

17

CHRISTMAS

*B*y anyone's standard, the way Christmas is celebrated today is a gross commercialism of the most important birth in history. We don't need to preach to the unsaved world to put Christ back into Christmas. They shouldn't; we should.

CHURCH BORROWING

*T*he church as a physical entity exists for just one purpose: to glorify God. It stands as the visible image of God's best, not subject to worldly compromise. It seems contradictory to profess the belief that God can heal the sick, feed the poor, transform the hearts of the corrupt, but can't supply the funds in advance with which to do these things.

COLLECTION

*G*od's principles of lending and collecting do not require a Christian to sit passively by if someone refuses to pay what is due. However, neither does it allow us to use the devices of the world to collect. There are boundaries within which we are to operate that are much narrower than those of the world. Christians will be tested in the area of collecting.

"The king. . .said. . .
'Here I forgave you all
that tremendous debt,
just because you asked me to—
shouldn't you have mercy
on others,
just as I had mercy on you?' "
(Matthew 18:32-33 TLB)

COMMITMENT

*T*he use of money is a very objective measure of our commitment to Jesus Christ and to His work. Christians who bypass God's work because they refuse even a slight discomfort have missed the mark.

"Commit your way to the Lord;
trust in him and he will. . .
make your righteousness
shine like the dawn,
the justice of your cause
like the noonday sun"
(Psalm 37:5-6 NIV).

COMMUNITY, CHRISTIAN

*C*are for the Christian community. I believe it is an abomination before God to see folks within the Christian community depending on welfare for support.

"[Ask] God to help you under-
stand what he wants you to do. . .
and [ask] that the way you live
will always please the Lord
and honor him, so that you will
always be doing good, kind
things for others"
(Colossians 1:9-10 TLB).

COMMUNITY, NON-CHRISTIAN

*W*e are directed to share with the non-Christian community. Ten times as many Scripture references pertain to sharing with nonbelievers as opposed to only Christians.

COMPROMISE

*T*here's a price to be paid for every compromise, especially to God's Word. That price is the loss of peace from God. Compromise at any level results in further compromise until finally the conscience is seared, and right and wrong are no longer distinguishable.

CONSCIENCE

*W*hether it's cheating on income taxes or telling a lie to sell a product or padding an expense account, a Christian must have a clear conscience regarding past business practices and personal dealings.

CONSOLIDATION

*C*onsolidation loans are tempting because you are able to pay off your creditors with the loan and then make one payment instead of several. Usually this just treats the "symptoms" for a while but not the problem.

"The rich rule over the poor, and the borrower is servant to the lender" (Proverbs 22:7 NIV).

CONTENTMENT

*T*he secret of a happy life is learning how to deal with both the good times and the bad and knowing how to be content with either.

"I know what it is to be in need, and I know what it is to have plenty. I have learned the secret of being content in any and every situation, whether well fed or hungry, whether living in plenty or in want" (Philippians 4:12 NIV).

CORRECTING PROBLEMS

*T*he real problems surrounding finances are usually related to three basic areas: ignorance, greed, and communications. So, to correct those problems, learn all you can about budgeting and keeping good records; remember that God wants you to have His best, so it's foolish to always want more than you have; and learn to talk to your mate about your needs, wants, and desires and work together to avoid the problems.

"After you [God] have corrected me I will thank you by living as I should! I will obey! Oh, don't forsake me and let me slip back into sin again" (Psalm 119:7-8 TLB).

COSIGNING

"He who is surety for a stranger will surely suffer for it, but he who hates going surety is safe" (Proverbs 11:15 NAS).

*C*osigning means to pledge your assets against the debts of someone else. Scripture specifically forbids this when it speaks of surety or striking of hands. Christians cosign either out of ignorance of what God's Word teaches or out of misguided conviction and guilt.

COUNSEL

"Plans go wrong with too few counselors; many counselors bring success" (Proverbs 15:22 TLB).

*M*any of us need assistance with establishing and maintaining a budget and working with creditors. Christian Financial Concepts operates a referral counselor network to link families in need of financial counsel with trained volunteer counselors in their local area.

COVETOUSNESS

"You shall not set your desire on your neighbor's house or land, his manservant or maidservant, his ox or donkey, or anything that belongs to your neighbor" (Deuteronomy 5:21 NIV).

*F*inancial bondage exists if a Christian looks at what others have and desires it. Covetousness should not characterize the Christian. Don't set your goals based on what others have.

CREDIT

Credit is the establishment of a mutual trust relationship between a lender and a borrower. The most common type of financial bondage is excessive use of credit.

*"The rich rules over the poor,
And the borrower becomes
the lender's slave"*
(Proverbs 22:7 NAS).

CREDIT CARDS

Credit and credit cards are not the problem; it is the misuse of credit that creates the problems. Four rules for using credits cards: never use them for anything except budgeted purchases; pay them off every month; the first month you cannot pay the bill off, destroy the card and never use it again; keep in mind that just because you can afford something, you don't necessarily need it.

*"Your strength must come
from the Lord's mighty power
within you. Put on all
of God's armor so that
you will be able to stand safe
against all strategies
and tricks of Satan"*
(Ephesians 6:10-11 TLB).

DANGER POINT

The danger point is when income barely equals outgo. If all the income is consumed in monthly expenses and something unexpected happens, such as the car breaking down, the result is additional indebtedness. A decision is necessary at this point: Make more money or spend less.

*"In his heart a man
plans his course,
but the Lord
determines his steps"*
(Proverbs 16:9 NIV).

DEBT, PERSONAL

*N*othing in the area of finances has so dominated or influenced the direction of our society during the last fifty years as much as debt. Debt is a condition that exists when there is a loan agreement. The fact that someone is in debt is the result of misunderstanding or disobeying God's principles.

"Beware, and be on your guard against every form of greed"
(Luke 12:15 NAS).

DEBT, CHURCH

*T*he average American church is as deeply in debt as the average American business—and with about the same rate of delinquent payments and bankruptcies. God's Word does not say that borrowing on the part of the church is forbidden. There are no absolutes. However, borrowing represents the least, rather than the best, for God's people.

"O Lord. . .this is your kingdom. Riches and honor come from you alone. . . . All of this material that we have gathered to build a temple for your holy name comes from you! It all belongs to you!"
(1 Chronicles 29:11-12, 16 TLB)

DEBT FREEDOM

*G*od's Word tells us that His plan for us is to be debt free. The blessings of becoming debt free go far beyond the financial area; they extend to the spiritual and marital realms. No one who is financially bound can be spiritually free.

"The Lord will open for you His good storehouse. . . to bless all the work of your hand; and you shall lend to many nations, but you shall not borrow"
(Deuteronomy 28:12 NAS).

DECEIT

*N*ot only did Abraham love and trust God, but he bowed his will to God's judgment. We must accept this concept of total stewardship because when we transfer assets or file bankruptcy to avoid creditors or deal deceitfully with creditors, we block God's channel for help. Deceit will financially bind and destroy peace and contentment.

"The heart is the most deceitful thing there is, and desperately wicked. . . . [The Lord] searches all hearts and examines deepest motives so he can give to each person his right reward, according to his deeds—how he has lived" (Jeremiah 17:9-10 TLB).

DECEPTION

*O*ne way we fail is to deceive ourselves into believing we're too strong to fail. The most devastating loss associated with deception is the dulling of spiritual awareness. Deception destroys trust and leads to hypocrisy and a critical spirit. God knew we wouldn't be perfect and made allowances for our weaknesses by a principle called confession.

"I will not allow those who deceive and lie to stay in my house. He who conceals his transgressions will not prosper, but he who confesses and forsakes them will find compassion" (Psalm 101:7 TLB, Proverbs 28:13 NAS).

DECISION MAKING

*T*here are biblical principles for financial decision making. Some of them are to: avoid speculation (assess every opportunity and do not let others make your decisions); keep your finances current (do not borrow beyond your ability to repay, even for one day); consider your witness (make every decision on the basis of its effect on the work and reputation of Christ); avoid indulgence (discern between needs, wants, and desires); and prepare for decreases.

DECREASES

*W*hen you make a financial decision, consider what would happen if you had even a small decrease in funds. Do not operate at the upper limit of your income; instead make decisions based on a reduced standard of living. Sometimes God's will is accomplished by a loss rather than a gain. The ability to thank God in every circumstance depends on full trust in Him.

DILIGENCE

*D*iligence is always necessary in financial matters, especially now, when the world has become so complex. We must watch over even the smallest of expenditures.

*"Poor is he who works
with a negligent hand,
but the hand of
the diligent makes rich"*
(Proverbs 10:4 NAS).

DISCERNMENT

*W*ebster's *Dictionary* describes discernment as the act of perceiving something hidden or concealed. God's Word more aptly defines it as the application of wisdom. Since all wisdom comes from God, we know that discernment means applying God's wisdom in discretionary matters.

*"If you want better insight
and discernment, and are
searching for them as you
would for lost money or hidden
treasure, then wisdom will be
given you, and knowledge
of God himself"*
(Proverbs 2:3-5 TLB).

DISCIPLESHIP

*S*ome Christian businesspeople, whose employees have never heard the gospel in a meaningful way, spend thousands of dollars a year to travel and share Christ with people in other countries. Christian business principles won't mean anything unless the unsaved see them in action. Unsaved employees have a tendency to believe what they see rather than what they hear.

*"And the things which you
have heard from me in the
presence of many witnesses,
these entrust to faithful men,
who will be able
to teach others also"*
(2 Timothy 2:2 NAS).

DISCIPLINE

*S*ometimes Christians apply a discipline to their business careers that is woefully lacking in their walk with the Lord. Christians are to be lights to lead others to Christ in a dark world. What we say is not enough. God requires that we "show and tell."

"Get wisdom, discipline and understanding. . . .Prove yourselves to be blameless and innocent, children of God above reproach in the midst of a crooked and perverse generation, among whom you appear as lights in the world"
(Proverbs 23:23 NIV,
(Philippians 2:15 NAS).

DISHONESTY

*C*an Christians be honest in our society? They must be to experience the fullness of God's power and love. Often there is a price to be paid for following in the path of Christ, but there is also a great reward as a result of doing so. No matter how successful dishonest people may seem to be, they will pay for their dishonesty in many ways. Following the worldly path results in the loss of God's full blessings.

"Do things in such a way that everyone can see you are honest clear through"
(Romans 12:17 TLB).

DIVERSIFICATION

*W*hen investing, there are no sure things; so the principle of diversification is essential to long-term stability. Divide your investment money into several parts and don't risk it all in one place. Diversify not only in different investments but also into differing areas of the economy.

*"Divide your portion to seven,
or even to eight,
for you do not know what
misfortune may occur
on the earth"*
(Ecclesiastes 11:2 NAS).

ECOLOGY

*E*verything we need has been given to us—food for ourselves and our flocks. How foolish we are when we destroy the land that supports us. We may "possess" the land, but God watches our actions carefully and will hold us responsible for any damage we may cause.

*"The Lord God took the man and
put him in the Garden of Eden to
work it and take care of it. I will
send rain on your land in its
season. . . .I will provide grass
in the fields for your cattle, and
you will eat and be satisfied"*
(Genesis 2:15,
Deuteronomy 11:14-15 NIV).

ECONOMY

*J*ust because the economy hasn't crashed yet doesn't mean it can't or won't. If enough of us believe it will and change our habits (and the government's), we might be able to avert it. I believe we are to use our minds in the service of our Lord.

*"The mind of man plans his
way, but the Lord
directs his steps"*
(Proverbs 16:9 NAS).

EGO

A Christian can excel at whatever he or she does without egotism. God desires to break our ego—not our spirit. We can accomplish a great deal in our own strength and ability, but the lasting effects are minimal.

EMPLOYEE RESPONSIBILITY

*J*ust as employers must stand responsible for their workers' welfare, employees have a responsibility to their vocational authority. Honor is the minimum attitude and excellence is the minimum standard acceptable to God.

EMPLOYER RESPONSIBILITY

*C*hristian employers and supervisors should be aware that authority is not a right; it is a responsibility. God established the principle that He will defend workers when they are wronged without cause. A Christian employer's long-range plans should include the welfare and advancement of the workers' interests.

ENDURANCE

*G*od knows what it takes to keep us attuned to His direction. He allows problems to occur that keep us dependent upon Him. If you want the perfecting of your faith, it comes by way of testing.

"Consider it all joy, my brethren, when you encounter various trials, knowing that the testing of your faith produces endurance" (James 1:2-3 NAS).

ENOUGH

*H*ow much is enough? Current provision is the composite of living standard and short-term cash reserves. No two families will have the same goals within God's will or the same standard of living. He has specific limits for us and those set our lifestyles.

"For the material they had was sufficient and more than enough for all the work, to perform it" (Exodus 36:7 NAS).

ENTANGLEMENTS

*E*ntanglements are the devious entrapments created by juggling the bills to keep afloat, and they are the worldly commitments that keep many Christians out of God's service: family loans, commercial borrowing, extra jobs, broken promises.

"The Lord is the Spirit, and where the Spirit of the Lord is, there is freedom. And we. . . are being transformed into his likeness with ever-increasing glory, which comes from the Lord, who is the Spirit" (2 Corinthians 3:17-18 NIV).

ENVY

*E*nvy is the desire to achieve based on observation of other people's successes. The wicked often do succeed in life, and the good often suffer, but it is foolishness to envy the success of the wicked when we could be building our own futures.

"Do not envy wicked men, do not desire their company. . . .Do not be overawed when a man grows rich, when the splendor of his house increases; for he will take nothing with him when he dies"
(Psalm 49:16-17,
Proverbs 24:1 NIV).

ETHICS

*M*any Christians are guilty of practicing situational ethics. They weigh what they see against God's Word and decide that it can't possibly mean what it says; therefore, to accomplish their goals, they reinterpret what the Word says. In other words, the situation determines the interpretation.

"Let us turn away from everything wrong, whether of body or spirit, and purify ourselves, living in the wholesome fear of God, giving ourselves to him alone"
(2 Corinthians 7:1 TLB).

EVIL

*W*e are told not to associate with evil people. The Bible warns us not even to eat with evil people. We should be very careful in all our associations with others, choosing wisely our business associates, employers, and friends.

"[Don't] keep company with anyone who claims to be a brother Christian but indulges in sexual sins, or is greedy, or is a swindler, or worships idols, or is a drunkard, or abusive. Don't even eat lunch with such a person"
(1 Corinthians 5:11 TLB).

EXCELLENCE

*W*e live in a society in which average is exceptional and slothful is normal. The trend today is to seek the path of least resistance and when the going gets difficult, give up. In school when grades are averaged together it's called "grading on the curve." We as Christians have allowed our standards to be graded by the "curve" of the world. It is vital that we walk according to God's Word.

"This plan of mine is not what you would work out. . . . As the heavens are higher than the earth, so are my ways higher than yours, and my thoughts than yours" (Isaiah 55:8-9 TLB).

EXCULPATE

*W*hen you exculpate a loan it means that the lender agrees to clear you of all blame (to hold you harmless) if for any reason you fail to pay the loan off according to the terms of the contract. When you sign any note payable and do not have an exculpatory clause, you have signed surety.

"Take his garment when he becomes surety for a stranger; and for foreigners, hold him in pledge" (Proverbs 20:16 NAS).

FAIRNESS

"You shall not oppress a hired servant who is poor and needy, whether he is one of your countrymen or one of your aliens who is in your land in your towns"
(Deuteronomy 24:14 NAS).

*T*he first step in establishing the principle of fairness is to recognize that all people are important, regardless of their vocational position. God is not concerned about what others think is fair but what He thinks is fair. You must pay employees a livable wage or hire those who can live on what you're able to pay.

FAITHFULNESS, GOD'S

"We stand true to the Lord whether others honor us or despise us, whether they criticize us or commend us. . . . Our hearts ache, but at the same time we have the joy of the Lord"
(2 Corinthians 6:8, 10 TLB).

*O*ne of the greatest joys a Christian can experience is God's faithfulness. He never fails us. Regardless of how other people treat us, God remains faithful.

FALSE GODS

"Beware, lest your hearts be deceived and you turn away and serve other gods and worship them. Or the anger of the Lord will be kindled against you"
(Deuteronomy 11:16-17 NAS).

*M*ost of us are not tempted to worship actual false gods made of gold and silver these days, but many of us do worship the gold and silver itself. Today's false gods are just as dangerous as those of times gone by, and we risk losing everything good God has put on this earth if we become entangled with modern-day false gods.

FAMILY

*G*od requires that we provide for our families. This provision for the family goes beyond just the husband, wife, and children. It includes others—mother, father, grandparents—right on down the line. It isn't the church's responsibility or that of the government. What kind of witnesses will we be to the non-Christian community if the members of our own families go without? Christians must awaken to this responsibility.

"But if anyone does not provide for his own, and especially for those of his household, he has denied the faith, and is worse than an unbeliever"
(1 Timothy 5:8 NAS).

FAVORITISM

*T*here should be no attitude of favoritism within the body of Christ. Many Christians and Christian organizations cater to wealthy individuals, and many wealthy Christians demand special attention. We are all the same in God's sight.

"How can you claim that you belong to the Lord Jesus Christ, the Lord of glory, if you show favoritism to rich people and look down on poor people?"
(James 2:1 TLB)

FEAR

*F*ear is a useless emotion. It paralyzes and imprisons. Evil is a reality but we cannot let it win. We have God's comfort and assurance. He gives us the confidence to go on in the face of evil, overcome fear, and walk bravely into the future, even though we do not know what we will find there.

"The Lord is my light and my salvation— whom shall I fear? The Lord is the stronghold of my life— of whom shall I be afraid? Though an army besiege me, my heart will not fear"
(Psalm 27:1,3 NIV).

FEAR OF GOD

"Blessed is the man who fears the Lord, who finds great delight in his commands" (Psalm 112:1 NIV).

Though we are taught to fear evil, fear of the Lord is another matter altogether. Fear of the Lord is living as the Lord instructs, and this will lead to prosperity and happiness.

FINANCIAL PLANNING

"A prudent man foresees the difficulties ahead and prepares for them; the simpleton goes blindly on and suffers the consequences" (Proverbs 22:3 TLB).

Planning is an essential element in any financial program, but particularly so for Christians. Often Christians question whether they should do any planning. They ask, "Shouldn't I depend totally on God?" Yes, but that doesn't mean to sit at home and wait for the delivery of manna. That is not God's attitude.

FIRSTFRUITS

"Honor the Lord with your wealth, with the firstfruits of all your crops; then your barns will be filled to overflowing, and your vats will brim over with new wine" (Proverbs 3:9-10 NIV).

The "firstfruits" belong to the Lord. That means right off of the top. It is only by honoring the Lord from the first part of our incomes (the gross) that God can take control.

FLEXIBILITY

*I*t's important to have plans and goals, but if you make plans that are inflexible, they will only hinder God's work because you won't be able to live with them. Develop plans that guide your financial life but also provide for some recreation and personal enjoyment as well.

"Be glad for all God is planning for you. Be patient in trouble, and prayerful always" (Romans 12:12 TLB).

FORECLOSURES

*A*lthough the bank foreclosing on your home is a serious problem, it does not mean God has washed His hands of you. You will learn a costly yet valuable lesson on the danger of surety. You are morally responsible for this debt. When you entered into your contract, you bound yourself by your word to fulfill its intent. Work out a payment plan for the balance.

"He who walks in integrity walks securely, But he who perverts his ways will be found out" (Proverbs 10:9 NAS).

FORGIVENESS

*T*he Bible teaches us to forgive. In financial matters, this is a hard command to obey. If our business competitor falls into hard times, are we big enough to give good advice? Can you forgive a debt someone owes you and can't pay? How far does forgiveness extend? As far as the Lord is concerned, it stretches without end.

"If your brother sins, rebuke him, and if he repents, forgive him. If he sins against you seven times in a day, and seven times comes back to you and says, 'I repent,' forgive him" (Luke 17:3-4 NIV).

FRAUD

*F*raud is prevalent in many sectors of the business community that involves both consumers and merchants, patients and doctors. God's Word says that deception will always be found out. Total honesty is the minimum acceptable standard for a Christian.

"He who walks in integrity walks securely, But he who perverts his ways will be found out" (Proverbs 10:9 NAS).

FREEDOM

*T*he steps to financial freedom are first to transfer ownership of every possession to God (this is essential to experience the Spirit-filled life in the area of finances). Then, get out of debt altogether. There is no greater sense of freedom than to owe no man any financial obligation.

"Let no debt remain outstanding, except the continuing debt to love one another" (Romans 13:8 NIV).

FRUGALITY

*J*ohn Wesley once said, "You cannot keep a devoted Christian poor. For by the very nature of God within him his frugalness will eventually make him successful." We have lost some of that frugality in our generation. We need to remember that we are merely managers of God's resources.

"Better is a little with righteousness than great income with injustice" (Proverbs 16:8 NAS).

FUTURE

*O*nly the Lord knows the future, and only the Lord has control over the future. However, by observing His principles we can make our future a whole lot less vexing. He would have all of us focus more on "today" and less on the uncertainty of the future.

*"Do not be anxious
for tomorrow;
for tomorrow will
care for itself.
Each day has enough trouble
of its own"*
(Matthew 6:34 NAS).

GAMBLING

*G*ambling is an almost irresistible enticement to those who desire to meet the wants and desires of family but cannot. A sin, according to God's Word, means missing the mark. Regardless of how socially acceptable the practice of gambling, it is preying on the weakness of others. If our value system is no better than the world's, then truly we have been conformed to the image of this world.

*"Do not conform any longer to
the pattern of this world,
but be transformed by the
renewing of your mind.
Then you will be able to test
and approve. . .his good,
pleasing and perfect will"*
(Romans 12:2 NIV).

GET RICH QUICK

*T*his attitude is characterized by attempts to make money quickly with little applied effort. An investment is a get-rich-quick program if an individual must make a hasty decision, assume excessive debt, borrow the money to invest, or deal deceitfully with people. Establish your standards by God's Word and seek good counsel.

GIFT GIVING

*T*he short-term gratification of gift giving won't balance the long-term stress of debt. It's only because of our indulgence-crazed society that children and parents have the unrealistic expectations they do today. We could all do some soul searching about the indulgent gifts we think others need.

GIFTS

*W*e have received special abilities or talents; we are encouraged to use them. Just as we are expected to be good stewards of our money, so we should be good stewards of God's gifts.

GIVING

*L*ike every other facet of serving God, all giving should be done with the right attitude. When giving is viewed as a rule and done out of a sense of duty, it becomes legalism. Giving in the hope that you will receive an abundance is also wrong. Giving beyond the tithe should be an outward material expression of a deeper spiritual commitment and an indication of a willing and obedient heart. Giving is a matter of growth and practice.

"If you give, you will get! Your gift will return to you in full and overflowing measure. It is more blessed to give than to receive" (Luke 6:38, Acts 20:35 TLB).

GOALS, SHORT-RANGE

*I*f your short-range goal is to make money, you should review it because it is not a Christian objective. Having money as a goal means you are depending on yourself and not on God. Instead, seek God's will and then achieve nothing less than excellence.

"Seek first his kingdom and his righteousness, and all these things will be given to you as well" (Matthew 6:33 NIV).

GOALS, LONG-RANGE

*A*ny financial plan for Christians should be in harmony with prayer-guided, long-range goals. Not every Christian will be wealthy but everyone has a responsibility to plan well, have good, sound objectives, and operate according to God's principles. Establish long-range goals only after much personal and family prayer.

*"In his heart
a man plans his course,
but the Lord
determines his steps"*
(Proverbs 16:9 NIV).

GOD'S CARE

*G*od provides for the flowers of the field and the birds of the air. Will He do less for us?

*"Consider the ravens:
They do not sow or reap, they
have no storeroom or barn; yet
God feeds them. And how much
more valuable you are than
birds! He will command his
angels concerning you to guard
you in all your ways"*
(Luke 12:24, Psalm 91:11 NIV).

GOD'S DIRECTION

*I*n every decision, accept that God guides your direction. Verify your decisions by checking them against God's Word, confirming them in prayer, and accepting His answers. There's nothing wrong with seeking His direction, but it is wrong to go your own way and then expect Him to bail you out.

*"Trust in the Lord with all your
heart, and do not lean on your
own understanding. In all your
ways acknowledge Him, and He
will make your paths straight"*
(Proverbs 3:5-6 NAS).

GOD'S WILL

*T*he key to realizing God's will in finances is a proper understanding of stewardship. God will not force His will on us, but once a Christian accepts the role of steward and manages God's resources according to His direction, God will entrust more and more to that person.

"Those who let themselves be controlled by their lower natures live only to please themselves, but those who follow after the Holy Spirit find themselves doing those things that please God" (Romans 8:5 TLB).

GOD'S WORD

*O*ne of the overwhelming characteristics of those who discern God's will for their lives is that they continually seek to put God first. We must keep our priorities in the correct order. Living by the Word of God is the best insurance policy in the world.

"Nothing is perfect except your words. Oh, how I love them. I think about them all day long. I will remain obedient to your Word" (Psalm 119:96-97, 101 TLB).

GOOD JUDGMENT

*T*oo often our decisions are based on our feelings, rather than God's direction. You may "feel" that God is directing you to do something, but if that something is contrary to God's Word it is the feeling that is wrong.

"The man who knows right from wrong and has good judgment and common sense is happier than the man who is immensely rich!" (Proverbs 3:13-14 TLB)

GRACE

"Now all praise to God for his wonderful kindness to us and his favor. . . .So overflowing is his kindness toward us that he took away all our sins through the blood of his Son, and he has showered down upon us the richness of his grace" (Ephesians 1:6-8 TLB).

*T*he law of grace means we're not compelled to do anything by virtue of a written law. It is unmerited and unearned favor. God will make all grace abound in each one of us.

GREED

"Be on your guard against all kinds of greed; a man's life does not consist in the abundance of his possessions" (Luke 12:15 NIV).

*G*reed has become such an accepted attitude that most major advertisements for luxury products are built around it. Greed is reflected when you always want the best or more than you have—even to the point of borrowing large amounts of money.

HELPING OTHERS

"It is God himself who has made us what we are and given us new lives from Christ Jesus; and long ages ago he planned that we should spend these lives in helping others" (Ephesians 2:10 TLB).

*A*n important aspect of God's work in our lives is to teach God's people to love and care about each other. We are admonished to love with deeds. It is the responsibility of each Christian to supply the needs of others who cannot do so for themselves.

HOARDING

*T*hose who use their money totally for self-satisfaction or hoard it for that elusive "rainy day" are just as financially bound in God's eyes as those in debt. A Christian cannot be within God's will and hoard money. Those who hoard try to rationalize their behavior with arguments that contradict God's Word.

"Even wise men die; the stupid and the senseless alike perish, and leave their wealth to others. Their inner thought is, that their houses are forever, and their dwelling places to all generations" (Psalm 49:10-11 NAS).

HOME LIFE

*F*rustration in the home life is reflected in the spiritual life. Most families have no plan for their finances and continue to borrow beyond their ability to repay. In these circumstances it is virtually impossible to be effective witnesses for Jesus Christ.

"A prudent man sees evil and hides himself, The naive proceed and pay the penalty" (Proverbs 27:12 NAS).

HONESTY

*N*ever allow yourself to be trapped into anything that is unethical, immoral, or dishonest, no matter how inviting it seems. There are no small lies—just lies. There are no small thefts—just thefts. A Christian's usefulness to God is directly proportional to his or her honesty.

"It is better to be poor than dishonest" (Proverbs 19:22 TLB).

HONOR

*"The reward of humility and
the fear of the Lord
are riches, honor and life"*
(Proverbs 22:4 NAS).

*T*he trend today is to seek the path of least resistance. The world has not conformed to God's standards, but rather to Satan's. It is vital that we walk according to God's Word. God's principles demand that, no matter what others are doing, we serve Him through every action we take.

HOPE

*"We rejoice in the hope of
the glory of God. And hope does
not disappoint us, because God
has poured out his love into
our hearts by the Holy Spirit,
whom he has given us"*
(Romans 5:2, 5 NIV).

You must decide what you believe and trust God regardless of the outside circumstances. In other words, "Keep on keeping on." God gave us many examples of people who faced difficult situations. Some collapsed into despair and self-pity, while others grew stronger. Those who grew strong were "doers of the Word and not hearers only."

HOSPITALITY

*I*n biblical times, hospitality meant feeding strangers and providing wanderers with a warm place to sleep—both for the preservation of life in a harsh land. Nowadays, few of us would even think of entertaining strangers in our homes. However, we can be witnesses by offering hospitality to new members of the church, visitors from another country, or the underprivileged.

"Don't forget to be kind to strangers, for some who have done this have entertained angels without realizing it! Cheerfully share your home with those who need a meal or a place to stay for the night" (Hebrews 13:2, 1 Peter 4:9 TLB).

HOUSING

*B*efore you decide whether to rent or buy a home, you must determine how much you can afford to spend for housing. If your job is not secure enough to take on a mortgage payment, consider renting for now. One of the essential foundation blocks of a biblically oriented financial plan is a debt-free home. It is yours, not the lender's.

"The prudent man considers his steps. . . . He blesses the dwelling of the righteous" (Proverbs 14:15, 3:33 NAS).

HUMILITY

*"Whoever exalts himself
shall be humbled;
and whoever humbles himself
shall be exalted"*
(Matthew 23:12 NAS).

*T*hough Christ is the most exalted being in the eternal kingdom of God, He assumed the lowliest, most humbling position possible during His lifetime. He not only served others, He also washed their feet.

IGNORANCE

*"He who trusts in himself
is a fool,
but he who walks in wisdom
is kept safe"*
(Proverbs 28:26 NIV).

*P*roblems with finances can stem from ignorance. Ignorance is not stupidity; it is a lack of understanding. Learn all you can, discipline your spending, and you'll be able to expand to the full measure of what God wants you to have.

IMPULSE BUYING

*"Don't begin until
you count the cost.
For who would begin
construction of a building
without first getting estimates
and then checking to see if he
has enough money
to pay the bills?"*
(Luke 14:28 TLB)

*I*f what you buy jeopardizes your financial freedom, forget it. Impulse buying, either for investment or consumption, is disastrous. When you evaluate a purchase, consider the obligation in light of your known income. Make every decision based on whether it may result in bondage.

INDEBTEDNESS

*D*ebt on consumables, such as food, clothing, and gasoline, is exceedingly difficult to repay. When they're gone, so is the desire to pay for them. What if you commit more of your income to creditors than you realistically can pay? Contact your creditors, be honest about your situation, and arrange some kind of equitable payment plan.

"The Lord lifts the fallen and those bent beneath their loads. The Lord is fair in everything he does, and full of kindness. He hears their cries for help and rescues them" (Psalm 145:14, 17-19 TLB).

INDULGENCE

*M*any Christians are frustrated because they can't distinguish between luxuries and necessities. Consequently, they seek fulfillment through the same channels as non-Christians and then wonder why they have a fruitless Christian walk. God wants us to live comfortably, but He does not want us to live lavishly when our resources could be used to promote God's work throughout the world.

"Do not love the world, nor the things in the world. For all that is in the world, the lust of the flesh and the lust of the eyes and the boastful pride of life, is not from the Father, but is from the world" (1 John 2:15-16 NAS).

INHERITANCE

*M*ost everyone has the ability to create an estate today. It may be land, a business, home, or an insurance policy payable upon death, but nevertheless it is an estate. Even a brief survey of the Bible reveals that God provided for each generation through inheritance. Being a good steward doesn't end with death. Develop a godly approach toward leaving an inheritance to your children and grandchildren.

*"A good man leaves
an inheritance
to his children's children,
And the wealth of the sinner is
stored up for the righteous"*
(Proverbs 13:22 NAS).

INSURANCE

*O*ften it is a misguided Christian who believes that having insurance is a lack of faith. Insurance can be used to an extreme and become the symbol of a lack of faith. But if used properly—to provide—it is good stewardship.

*"Our aim is to please him
always in everything we do,
whether we are here in this
body or away from this body
and with him in heaven"*
(2 Corinthians 5:9 TLB).

INTEREST

*I*n regard to lending to others, God's Word says that we should not charge interest to those within God's family—it is a demonstration that God can provide without charging interest to one another; but we can charge interest to nonbelievers.

*"You may charge interest
to a foreigner, but to your
countryman you shall not
charge interest"*
(Deuteronomy 23:20 NAS).

INVESTING

*I*nvesting is found in both the Old Testament (Adam planted seeds that could have been eaten and became an investor) and the New Testament (the parable of the talents). If investing were prohibited, why would Jesus use it as an example and reward the most diligent? Investing is just another part of stewardship—not more important than giving but not less important either.

"There is precious treasure and oil in the dwelling of the wise, but a foolish man swallows it up" (Proverbs 21:20 NAS).

IRRESPONSIBILITY

*T*here's a definite difference between a Christian who is financially bound because of irresponsibility and one who can't meet family needs because of circumstances such as injury or illness. The kind of bondage that occurs because of bad habits and an unwillingness to meet the needs of others is called irresponsibility.

"These people honor me with their lips, but their hearts are far from me. They worship me in vain; their teachings are but rules taught by men" (Matthew 15:8-9 NIV).

JEALOUSY

*T*o look at what others have and admire it is called appreciation. To look at what others have and desire it is called covetousness. To look at what others have and resent it is called sin.

"Wherever there is jealousy or selfish ambition, there will be disorder and every other kind of evil" (James 3:16 TLB).

JUDGING OTHERS

"You have no right to criticize your brother or look down on him. Remember, each of us will stand personally before the Judgment Seat of God"
(Romans 14:10 TLB).

*T*he standards by which we are to judge one another are really very simple; they're called the Ten Commandments. Anything other than this is just an opinion.

JUSTICE

"There is no truer statement than this: God is never wicked or unjust. He alone has authority over the earth and dispenses justice for the world"
(Job 34:12-13 TLB).

*T*o question why the unrighteous aren't punished by God is to question His wisdom. After all, this life is the only heaven they will ever experience.

LAWSUITS

"Actually, then, it is already a defeat for you, that you have lawsuits with one another. Why not rather be wronged? Why not rather be defrauded?"
(1 Corinthians 6:7 NAS)

*A*lthough a believer is instructed not to sue another for personal loss, the same is not true for criminal action. By law a criminal act is committed against the whole of society. It's important to bear in mind that God's Word deals much more with our attitudes than with our actions.

LAZINESS

*I*n his travels the apostle Paul found many Christians who had no desire to work but rather relied on the brethren to take care of them. Each of us must have the desire to work if we are to accomplish what God put us on this earth to do. Financial bondage exists when there is no desire for gainful employment.

"If anyone will not work, neither let him eat" (2 Thessalonians 3:10 NAS).

LEGALISM

*T*he Pharisees did what they thought was right—prayed, fasted, tithed. Christ never challenged their actions; He challenged their motives. They were so blinded by their own self-righteousness they couldn't see God's true promises.

"You pay tithe of mint and rue and every kind of garden herb, and yet disregard justice and the love of God; but these are the things you should have done without neglecting the others" (Luke 11:42 NAS).

LENDING

*T*here's no record of a society that operated for any period of time without borrowing and lending. Lending is not prohibited scripturally. It's interesting that lending is one of the blessings promised by God for being obedient to His ways.

"The Lord will open for you His good storehouse. . .and you shall lend to many nations, but you shall not borrow" (Deuteronomy 28:12 NAS).

LEVERAGE

*W*hen investing, avoid the use of leverage—the ability to control a large asset with a relatively small investment. If you buy property for $10,000 and pay $1,000 down, that's a nine-to-one lever. You invested 10 percent of your money and borrowed 90 percent. Borrowing money to invest is not a scriptural principle.

LIFESTYLE

*G*od will not use money to allow us to satisfy our every whim and desire. It is important that we begin to adjust to lifestyles compatible with Christian commitment. God does not want us to live in poverty but neither does He want us to live lavishly while His work needs money and other Christians go without food and clothing.

LOSS

*T*here is little question that a totally honest businessperson will experience some losses and will be misused by others, at least in the short run. But God will compensate for any losses in many ways, not the least of which is supernatural peace.

LOYALTY

*L*oyalty can be defined as absolute commitment even in the face of adversity. By that definition, loyalty is a rare commodity today. Remember, loyalty begets loyalty. God's Word supports honoring those who are loyal.

*"Many a man proclaims
his own loyalty,
but who can find
a trustworthy man?"*
(Proverbs 20:6 NAS)

MAKING DECISIONS

*B*e certain that the affairs and decisions of each day are surrendered to God. The essential elements in making sound financial decisions are adequate knowledge and the wisdom to apply it.

*"The wisdom that comes from
heaven is first of all pure and full
of quiet gentleness. . .
it is peace-loving and courteous.
It allows discussion and
is willing to yield to others"*
(James 3:17 TLB).

MARRIAGE

*T*he effects of financial bondage on a marriage relationship are measurable in the statistics of failed marriages. A marriage should be a partnership—much like the right and left hands of the same person. God's Word says that two people become one.

*"For this cause a man shall leave
his father and his mother, and
shall cleave to his wife; and they
shall become one flesh"*
(Genesis 2:24 NAS).

MATERIALISM

"A man's life does not consist in the abundance of his possessions" (Luke 12:15 NIV).

*T*he initial purpose of material things is to make our lives easier and more comfortable. But it's amazing how complicated they can become. In fact, the urgency of our materialistic lifestyles becomes a tyranny that demands most of our energies.

MEDIOCRITY

"Do you see a man skilled in his work?. . . He will not stand before obscure men" (Proverbs 22:29 NAS).

*W*e have found it easier to adjust to mediocrity than the source of excellence—God's Word. Therefore, it is vital that we walk according to His Word; reassess our basic attitudes; recognize that if we don't conform to God's standards, we have conformed to Satan's. In order to avoid mediocrity, we must recognize the fallacy of the world's standards.

MERCY

"Surround me with your tender mercies, that I may live. For your law is my delight" (Psalm 119:77 TLB).

*E*ven though Job suffered tremendous losses, he remained faithful and God had mercy on him, restoring all Job had lost. In hard times we need the patience Job had, but we should never forget that our God is a God of mercy and has rewards waiting for us if we remain faithful.

MONEY, LOVE OF

*W*hen we love money and order our lives around its accumulation and preservation, we have made money our god, putting it before everything else and guaranteeing that we will not live a righteous life. If we put God and His commands first, then we are free to pursue success, knowing that we have our priorities in the right order and God will reward us.

"The love of money is a root of all kinds of evil. Some people, eager for money, have wandered from the faith and pierced themselves with many griefs"
(1 Timothy 6:10 NIV).

NEEDY

*D*o you turn your face away when you see a homeless person huddling in a doorway? Even if our society manages to solve the dilemma of the homeless, there still will be others in need. The verse is specific enough in what it's saying. It is a command. There's no choice involved; if you follow God, you will give to the needy.

"There will always be poor people in the land. Therefore I command you to be openhanded toward your brothers and toward the poor and needy in your land"
(Deuteronomy 15:11 NIV).

OBEDIENCE

*S*ince finances is one of the most often discussed topics in the New Testament, it would seem obvious that God would use that area to test our obedience to Him. Each Christian must come to the position where God's approval is more important than the world's riches. Then, and only then, will the full measure of God's peace and power be experienced.

"God blesses those who obey him; happy the man who puts his trust in the Lord"
(Proverbs 16:20 TLB).

OBEY THE LAW

*G*od demands obedience to the law. Many Christians rationalize their violation of the tax laws. People who wouldn't think of robbing a bank justify stealing from the government. Take maximum advantage of every tax law in existence but be careful not to cross the line and become involved in tax evasion and theft.

"He who profits illicitly troubles his own house, but he who hates bribes will live"
(Proverbs 15:27 NAS).

OBSTACLES

Obstacles to good financial planning include the following: social pressures to own more "things"; the attitude that "more is better" regardless of cost; use of credit to delay necessary decisions; no surplus available to cope with rising prices and unexpected expenses. Don't offset increases in income by increasing your level of spending.

"Put off your old self,
which is being corrupted
by its deceitful desires;
to be made new in
the attitude of your minds"
(Ephesians 4:22-23 NIV).

OPPRESSION

Who is an oppressor today? Isn't the housewife who pays an illegal alien less than minimum wage oppressing that worker? Isn't the businessperson who sends manufacturing overseas because of cheap labor oppressing workers both there and at home? The ends never justify the means, especially when the means involve profiting from the oppression of other people.

"All who are oppressed
may come to him.
He is a refuge for them
in their times of trouble"
(Psalm 9:9 TLB).

ORGANIZATION

In business, organization is an absolute necessity, not an alternative. A smart entrepreneur will learn that although ideas start businesses, organization makes them successful. That means a business owner must either develop the necessary discipline or hire someone else to keep the company in order.

"Poor is he who works with a negligent hand, but the hand of the diligent makes rich" (Proverbs 10:4 NAS).

OVERCOMMITMENT

Of all the problems that cause financial friction, probably none is more disheartening to a wife than a husband overcommitted to his work. And some women are so wrapped up in their work that they have little or no time for family. There is a balance in life between hard work and enjoying life, and the wise person does both.

"Do not wear yourself out to get rich; have the wisdom to show restraint" (Proverbs 23:4 NIV).

OVERDRAFT

*M*any banks offer an automatic overdraft protection service—if you write a check in excess of what you have in your account, the bank will still honor it. This looks like a helpful service. However, it tends to create a complacent attitude about balancing the account and encourages overdrafting, which adds charges to your account.

"Now it is required that those who have been given a trust must prove faithful" (1 Corinthians 4:2 NIV).

OWNERSHIP, GOD'S

*O*nce you accept the fact that God owns everything it's important to manage all you have according to His rules. It's how you manage money that determines how you will manage greater things.

"For we have brought nothing into the world, so we cannot take anything out of it either" (1 Timothy 6:7 NAS).

OWNERSHIP, PERSONAL

A Christian must transfer ownership of every possession to God—money, time, family, material possessions, education, even earning potential for the future. If we make a total transfer of everything to God, He will demonstrate His perfect will in our lives.

"Since he did not spare even his own Son for us but gave him up for us all, won't he also surely give us everything else?" (Romans 8:32 TLB)

PARTNERSHIPS

*"Don't be teamed with those who
do not love the Lord,
for what do the people of God
have in common
with the people of sin?"*
(2 Corinthians 6:14 TLB)

*P*eople with opposite goals and values will not be compatible. When they are linked together in business their differing values will ultimately create conflicts. Christians are admonished not to be yoked together with unbelievers.

PATIENCE

*"When your patience is
finally in full bloom,
then you will be ready
for anything"*
(James 1:4 TLB).

*F*rom the time we're born we want what we want when we want it. We tend to run out and get what we want, or if it can't be bought, then we lose patience. God can't be rushed. He hears us and when the time is right He will provide.

PEACE

*"My peace I give you.
I do not give to you
as the world gives.
Do not let your hearts
be troubled and
do not be afraid"*
(John 14:27 NIV).

*T*he world has the power to prevent us from getting ahead financially, to destroy our spirits, and even to kill us, but if our faith in God is firm nothing the world can do to us can destroy our inner peace.

PERSISTENCE

*I*f God's people give up too easily when faced with difficulties, the world will consider us losers. Nothing and nobody can shake a true believer from doing God's will once it is understood. Be persistent in the face of problems.

*"If you keep knocking long enough he will get up and give you everything you want—
just because of your persistence.
And so it is with prayer—
keep on asking and
you will keep on getting"*
(Luke 11:8-9 TLB).

PERSEVERANCE

*P*erseverance is a characteristic lacking in Christianity today. Some Christians who fail get defeated and feel like God has abandoned them. We must believe that God wants to bless us, and until God individually convicts us that our plan is otherwise, we are not to accept failure.

*"Without faith it is impossible
to please Him,
for he who comes to God
must believe that He is,
and that He is a rewarder
of those who seek Him"*
(Hebrews 11:6 NAS).

PLANNING

*W*e can plan and plan and never see any of our plans work out the way we had hoped. Or we can read God's Word, listen to His advice, live the way He tells us to, plan what and when He tells us to plan, and reap the benefits.

*"I will instruct you and teach you
in the way you should go;
I will counsel you and
watch over you"*
(Psalm 32:8 NIV).

POVERTY

*F*olklore suggests that poverty is next to spirituality. Wrong! There's no inherent virtue in poverty. There are dishonest poor just as there are dishonest rich. God never impoverished anyone because of his or her spirituality. Therefore, there is no way Christians can attain spirituality by impoverishing themselves or their families.

PRAISE

*T*o get the praise of others is not difficult. Just do what they want, when they want it, and how they want. The trick is guessing what, when, and how. One bad guess and the praise is gone.

PRAYER

*P*rayer is a gift, but it should not be misused. Christ asked His Father to bless His work on earth. And when Christ left this earth, He passed that responsibility along to us. Using the name of Jesus in prayer can bring into our hands all that God has for us. (The key to prayer is in Mark 11:22-25).

Prenuptial Agreements

*T*hese agreements, between two people contemplating marriage, are becoming more common in a society that plans for divorce before marriage begins. To do this merely allows Satan a foothold in the marriage that he will exercise at his leisure.

"Be imitators of God, therefore, as dearly loved children and live a life of love, just as Christ loved us and gave himself up for us as a fragrant offering and sacrifice to God" (Ephesians 5:1-2 NIV).

Pride

*P*ride is perhaps the major sin in Christendom today. Pride—the desire to be first—leads to greed—a craving for more. Pride is so deceptive because it's so normal today. The way to deal with pride is to consciously put others first.

"Everyone who is proud in heart is an abomination to the Lord. Pride goes before destruction, and a haughty spirit before stumbling" (Proverbs 16:5,18 NAS).

Priorities

*T*he decay of a Christian's spiritual life usually can be traced directly to incorrect priorities. Almost without exception, these misplaced priorities relate to money. Money and its related symptoms (pride, greed, ego) divert our affections from God.

"You cannot serve God and mammon" (Luke 16:13 NAS).

PROFIT, BUSINESS

*P*rofits are the economic rewards of good service and products. Every Christian in business—employer and employee alike—should work to maximize profits, but not to the exclusion of the other elements of a biblically based business. To maximize profits by underpaying employees is a violation of God's principles for business.

PROFIT, PERSONAL

*T*he keys to generating a profit according to the principles in God's Word are not complicated. Seek godly counsel and acknowledge and obey God's eternal wisdom in operating your business. Too often, we seek God's wisdom and then violate the principles taught in His Word.

PROMISES

*W*hen God promises us things, He promises them through His Word. And the Bible has in it everything God will ever do for us. What God promises in Scripture, He delivers.

PROPERTY

*M*ost business owners go to great lengths to reduce and eliminate employee misuse of company property (pens, pencils, paper, copies). It's estimated that employee theft accounts for the loss of nearly $160 billion per year. Business owners tend to believe they can treat company property as their own (company vehicles, telephone use), but to do so constitutes sin.

"Do not enter the path of the wicked, and do not proceed in the way of evil men" (Proverbs 4:14 NAS).

PROSPERITY

*G*od is not against prosperity. The Scriptures give evidence that one of God's blessings to those who love and obey Him is prosperity. By listening to God's teachings, we gain both emotional and physical security, which leaves us free to live a happy and prosperous life.

"Blessed are all who fear the Lord, who walk in his ways. You will eat the fruit of your labor; blessings and prosperity will be yours" (Psalm 128:1-2 NIV).

PROVISION

*"Go to the ant, O sluggard, observe
her ways and be wise, which,
having no chief, officer or ruler,
prepares her food in the summer,
and gathers her provision
in the harvest"*
(Proverbs 6:6-8 NAS).

*I*f we are slack and do not earn our way, poverty
will come upon us and our families. Neglect
occurs when we have the capability of supplying
our family's needs but fail to do so. God will provide for our needs beyond any doubt. But we have
the requirement from God to be prudent.

PRUDENCE

*"A simple man believes anything,
but a prudent man gives
thought to his steps.
A prudent man sees danger
and takes refuge,
but the simple keep going
and suffer for it"*
(Proverbs 14:15, 22:3 NIV).

*S*ometimes it seems there's too much advice
around: your brother-in-law made a fortune
investing; your cousin did well with bonds; Aunt
Millie prefers the neighborhood bank. Only the
foolish would take free advice without looking
into it carefully, weighing all the risks, and then
making an informed decision.

RELATIONSHIPS

*"Wives, submit to your husbands. . . .
Husbands, love your wives. . . .
Children, obey your parents. . . .
Fathers, do not
embitter your children. . . .
Slaves, obey your earthly masters. . . .
Masters, provide your slaves with
what is right and fair"*
(Colossians 3:18-22, 4:1 NIV).

*T*he chain of relationships from family to work
is so intertwined that the apostle Paul listed them
as a series in Colossians: husband-wife; parent-
child; and authority-work. Paul knew that unless
a Christian had all these managed properly, his or
her life could not manifest joy, peace, or contentment.

REMARRIAGE, WIDOWS

*T*ime has a way of healing wounds. There's no reason why a widow should not remarry, assuming it is the Lord's will. God designed people to live in pairs, with few exceptions.

"Two are better than one because they have a good return for their labor. For if either of them falls, the one will lift up his companion" (Ecclesiastes 4:9-10 NAS).

RENEWAL

*S*ince most financial problems stem from spiritual problems, the solution must be spiritual. The only source of spiritual renewal is from the Holy Spirit. Examine your spiritual life honestly.

"Do not be conformed to this world, but be transformed by the renewing of your mind, that you may prove what the will of God is, that which is good and acceptable and perfect" (Romans 12:2 NAS).

REPUTATION

*A*lthough God is faithful to forgive us when we ask forgiveness for violating His principles of finance, that does not mean we can avoid the consequences of our actions. It takes a long time to build up a good reputation but little to destroy it.

"A good reputation is more valuable than the most expensive perfume" (Ecclesiastes 7:1 TLB).

RESCUE

*"Our God whom we serve
is able to deliver us. . . .
But even if He does not. . .
we are not going to serve
your gods or worship
the golden image"*
(Daniel 3:17-18 NAS).

*S*hadrach, Meshach, and Abed-nego said that even if God didn't rescue them from the fiery furnace they would remain faithful to God. They confirmed a biblical principle: God may rescue us, or He may not, but it should make no difference in our obedience to Him and His Word.

RESENTMENT

*"You are those who justify
yourselves in the sight of men, but
God knows your hearts;
for that which is highly esteemed
among men is detestable in the
sight of God"*
(Luke 16:15 NAS).

Those who are resentful about the success of others, whose feelings are hurt because of the lack of recognition, or who use a job as their alter egos all suffer from the spiritual malady—they are serving men instead of God.

RESPONSIBILITY

*"The Lord's blessing is
our greatest wealth.
All our work adds
nothing to it!"*
(Proverbs 10:22 TLB)

*T*o be responsible means to be accountable for our actions. Christ said His followers must be willing to surrender their rights and follow His example. It's inconceivable that He would ever strike a deal and then back out to negotiate a better deal. Nor is it believable that He would run up a bill and then back out of paying it.

RESTITUTION

*W*henever you detect a deception in your own life, large or small, stop what you're doing and confess it immediately, not only to God but to others who are involved. And, even if you must suffer a financial loss to correct an earlier deception, then do whatever is necessary. Confession of a sin is not all that is required. Restitution should be made whenever possible.

"He who conceals his transgressions will not prosper, but he who confesses and forsakes them will find compassion" (Proverbs 28:13 NAS).

RETIREMENT

*R*etirement for Christians should mean freeing time to devote to serving others more fully without the necessity of getting paid for it. If Christian retirees have this motivation in mind while looking forward to retirement, then the Lord really will find us doing His work when He returns.

"By wisdom a house is built, and by understanding it is established; and by knowledge the rooms are filled with all precious and pleasant riches" (Proverbs 24:3-4 NAS).

REVENGE

*"Don't say, 'Now I can pay him
back for all his meanness to me!'
For we know him who said,
'Justice belongs to me;
I will repay them'"*
(Proverbs 24:29,
Hebrews 10:30 TLB).

*T*oo often we harbor resentment in our hearts when someone offends or cheats us. The reason the Lord tells us that revenge belongs to Him is so we can be free of resentment, anger, and frustration, as well as the need for getting even.

REVERENCE

*"The Angel of the Lord guards and
rescues all who reverence him.
If you belong to the Lord,
reverence him"*
(Psalm 34:7 TLB).

*W*ebster's Dictionary defines reverence as "profound, adoring, awed respect." I question how many Christians really stand in awe of the Lord today. Without awe, no one can truly reverence the Creator.

RICHES

*"Some rich people are poor,
and some poor people
have great wealth!"*
(Proverbs 13:7 TLB)

*T*hose whose most important possession is money will always have something to worry and complain about. Those whose most important possessions are family, love, service, and the Lord, are secure and happy in their riches. Only the rich have to get up early to check the stock market and stay up late to count their money and find a good hiding place for it.

RIGHTEOUSNESS

*R*ighteous people receive so many blessings that there will be plenty left over to pass on to their children and grandchildren; but sinners who become wealthy will see their riches being used by the righteous and will have nothing to leave to their children.

"He who walks in his uprightness fears the Lord. Better is a little with righteousness than great income with injustice" (Proverbs 14:2, 16:8 NAS).

RISK

*I*f you are going to invest, you will assume some risk. The general rule is, the greater the potential return, the greater the potential risk. Those who take excessive risks, however, do so because they lack the knowledge and ability to evaluate the actual risk.

"The plans of the diligent lead surely to advantage, but everyone who is hasty comes surely to poverty" (Proverbs 21:5 NAS).

SACRIFICE

*T*he concept of sacrifice is not popular with most Christians. Most of us like to discuss this subject in generalities rather than specifics. Those who have truly surrendered their finances to God also experience His faithfulness. Jesus promised something to those making sacrifices.

"Everyone who has left houses or brothers or sisters or father or mother or children or fields for my sake will receive a hundred times as much and will inherit eternal life" (Matthew 19:29 NIV).

SACRIFICIAL GIVING

"Anyone who oppresses the poor is insulting God who made them. To help the poor is to honor God" (Proverbs 14:31 TLB).

*T*his means of giving is available to Christians absolutely committed to God's plan. Often our level of commitment is to provide the needy with a ride to the welfare office. God will not allow His work to tarry for lack of funds. He will simply redistribute the necessary funds to Christians who will sacrifice personal luxuries for the needs of others.

SAVINGS

"The wise man saves for the future, but the foolish man spends whatever he gets" (Proverbs 21:20 TLB).

*I*t is not unspiritual to save; nor does it represent a lack of faith. It's important that you budget some savings. Otherwise, the use of credit becomes a lifelong necessity and debt a way of life. Your savings will allow you to purchase with cash and shop for the best buys.

SECURITY

Sometimes we see God as stern and strict, a parent who lays down law after law that we can't possibly obey. But above all, He is our loving parent, and just as we want our own children to be happy above everything else, so important is our happiness to our Heavenly Father.

"I have set the Lord always before me. Because he is at my right hand, I will not be shaken" (Psalm 16:8 NIV).

....

SELF-CONTROL

You can live well—and in this country we do live very well—but it is important that there be a difference in our commitment as compared to the nonbeliever. As the Holy Spirit convicts you, ask yourself: "Is there a difference between my lifestyle and the nonbeliever's?"

"Those controlled by the sinful nature cannot please God. You, however, are controlled not by the sinful nature but by the Spirit, if the Spirit of God lives in you" (Romans 8:8-9 NIV).

....

SELF-DENIAL

It is a contrast in human logic that by giving up something we can receive even more. But Christ taught this principle frequently; it's called sowing and reaping. It is our choice whether to take what we want now or store it and receive it in God's eternal kingdom. When you compare the time to enjoy God's rewards to the time spent in this world, there is no contest.

"If anyone wishes to come after Me, let him deny himself, and take up his cross daily, and follow Me" (Luke 9:23 NAS).

SELF-DISCIPLINE

"I will let every one who conquers sit beside me on my throne, just as I took my place with my Father on his throne when I had conquered" (Revelation 3:21 TLB).

A Christian must learn self-discipline with money to be able to teach others. Overcome your impulses to buy. If you haven't budgeted for it, don't buy it. Base your decisions upon the principles of God's Word—not the world's conventional wisdom.

SELF-ESTEEM

"What profit is there in gaining the whole world when it means forfeiting one's self?" (Luke 9:25 TLB)

*T*hose who accumulate money for self-esteem do so that others might envy them. This is a worldly motive, yet it characterizes many Christians. A Christian cannot accumulate for self-esteem within God's plan. Esteem and importance will fade as quickly as the money. Are you working for the esteem of others or the rewards of God?

SELF-INDULGENCE

*I*t's easy to rationalize a self-indulgent lifestyle in a society in which most people indulge themselves. To get the right balance, we must go to God's Word. It is not necessary to live poorly to serve the Lord. The only people who think poverty is spiritual are those who haven't tried it. But, affluence is perhaps the greatest threat to our walk with the Lord.

"For where your treasure is, there will your heart be also" (Matthew 6:21 NAS).

SELFISHNESS

*T*he theology of selfishness is an easy one to promote because most of us were raised with it, and today it virtually dominates our society. It's the philosophy called "get all you can out of life today—go for the gusto." That isn't a new philosophy. Solomon described it in the book of Ecclesiastes.

"Do nothing from selfishness or empty conceit, but with humility of mind let each of you regard one another as more important than himself" (Philippians 2:3 NAS).

SHARING

*T*he decision to share with others may not make sense to the world. We share out of obedience to God's Word; it says we are to help others. We accept the needs of others as our own. Anyone who gives willingly receives a blessing that comes only with true love. God will honor your attitude more than the amount.

"When you did it to these my brothers you were doing it to me! When you refused to help the least of these my brothers, you were refusing help to me"
(Matthew 25:40,45 TLB).

SINGLE PARENTS

*M*ost Christians have been blinded to the needs of single parents. They somehow think that the government provides all their needs. Not so. Single parents don't need welfare; they need friends who care. The only long-term solution to the dilemma of single parents is a good job with adequate pay.

"Share each other's troubles and problems, and so obey our Lord's command. And let us not get tired of doing what is right, for after a while we will reap a harvest of blessing"
(Galatians 6:2,9 TLB).

SINNING

*S*inning against a person doesn't have to involve stealing or ruining his or her possessions. We can also steal a person's reputation or destroy that person's self-confidence with poorly chosen words. We should confess all sin and do our best to rectify any problems we have caused.

"He who conceals his transgressions will not prosper, but he who confesses and forsakes them will find compassion"
(Proverbs 28:13 NAS).

SLANDER

*I*n one college class the professor had the students sit in a circle and pass along a rumor he had started. By the time it made its way back to him, it was a confirmed fact and greatly exaggerated. Try it in your Sunday school class some time.

"Anyone who refuses to slander others, does not listen to gossip, never harms his neighbor, speaks out against sin. . .such a man shall stand firm forever" (Psalm 15:3-5 TLB).

SLOTHFULNESS

*G*od thoroughly disapproves of slothfulness on our part and expects multiplication of the assets He leaves us, not just maintenance. Slothfulness means that we're willing to get by with less than our individual best. The opposite of slothfulness is not busyness—it is excellence!

"Never be lazy in your work but serve the Lord enthusiastically" (Romans 12:11 TLB).

SPECULATION

*E*very Christian should seek God's increase and make no provision for speculative schemes. Many times enticing programs are not only unethical but border on being illegal. Assess every opportunity in relation to your own commitment to Christ. Make your decision in light of your goals; evaluate whether a venture is necessary.

"What advantage has a wise man over a fool? Better what the eye sees than the roving of the appetite. This too is meaningless, a chasing after the wind" (Ecclesiastes 6:8-9 NIV).

SPIRITUAL VALUES

"He who is faithful in a very little thing is faithful also in much" (Luke 16:10 NAS).

God's Word teaches that the way we handle our money is the clearest reflection of our spiritual value system.

STEWARDSHIP

"Now it is required that those who have been given a trust must prove faithful" (1 Corinthians 4:2 NIV).

Christians have become victims of one of the most devious plots Satan ever created—the concept that money belongs to us and not to God. Indeed, everything we own belongs to God—including money. We cannot experience peace in the area of finances until we have surrendered total control of this area to God and accepted our position as stewards. God is the owner. We are the stewards.

STRENGTH

"For the eyes of the Lord range throughout the earth to strengthen those whose hearts are fully committed to him" (2 Chronicles 16:9 NIV).

Strength does not always mean the exercise of power. More often it means relinquishing personal rights to God. The opposite of strength is cowardice, which is generally motivated by self-preservation, not compassion. Strength, then, is the proper use of power to accomplish God's assigned tasks.

SUCCESS

*G*od's plan for success is unique for each individual, but it is common in that He never provides success at the expense of serving Him first, at the expense of peace, or at the expense of the family. The Scriptures reveal that the truly successful servants of the Lord made decisions on the preconditioned belief that God's way wasn't just the best way—it was the only way.

"In everything you do,
put God first,
and he will direct you and crown
your efforts with success"
(Proverbs 3:6 TLB).

SUPERIORITY

*Y*ou'd think that knowing everything belongs to God would make even the wealthiest among us humble. But it's sad what a little bit of success will do to our egos and pride. Those who have been given responsibility in this life must be very careful to exercise it with great caution, lest they give up their eternal rewards for some temporary ones.

"When others are happy,
be happy with them.
If they are sad,
share their sorrow.
Don't try to act big. . .
and don't think you know it all!"
(Romans 12:15-16 TLB)

SURETY

"A man lacking in sense pledges, and becomes surety in the presence of his neighbor" (Proverbs 17:18 NAS).

*S*urety means to deposit a pledge in either money, goods, or part payment for a greater obligation. It means taking on an obligation to pay later without a sure and certain way to pay. Surety is not a biblical law; it is a principle. If you violate the principle, you suffer the consequences.

SURPLUS

"Because of the proof given by this ministry they will glorify God for your obedience. . . and for the liberality of your contribution to them and to all" (2 Corinthians 9:13 NAS).

*G*od has commissioned us to help Christians to be better stewards, and that includes using surplus resources properly. It's obvious that those with a surplus are able to give more to God's work than others are.

TAXES

"Render to all what is due them: tax to whom tax is due; custom to whom custom; fear to whom fear; honor to whom honor" (Romans 13:7 NAS).

*G*od demands obedience to the law—and that includes tax laws. Some people rationalize their violation of tax laws. People who would not think of robbing a bank try to justify stealing from the government.

TEMPTATION

*L*ife is full of temptation, but there are "seasons" when it seems that temptations are everywhere: cheat a little on taxes, charge a little more than is necessary, pad an expense account.

*"No temptation is irresistible.
[God] will show you how to
escape temptation's power
so that you can bear up
patiently against it"*
(1 Corinthians 10:13 TLB).

THANKFULNESS

*I*t is remarkable that in America we could ever think that God has failed us materially. That attitude is possible only when we allow Satan to convince us to compare ourselves to others. The primary defense against this attitude is praise to God. Until we can truly thank God for what we have and be willing to accept that as God's provision for our lives, contentment will never be possible.

*"O Lord, Thou art my God;
I will exalt Thee,
I will give thanks to Thy name;
for Thou hast worked wonders,
plans formed long ago,
with perfect faithfulness"*
(Isaiah 25:1 NAS).

THINGS

*"The world and
its desires pass away,
but the man who does the will
of God lives forever"*
(1 John 2:17 NIV).

*T*he initial purpose of material things is to make our lives easier and more comfortable; however, the possession of "things" has become the scorecard to determine success. The pressure to provide the luxuries that now have become commonplace causes many of us to encumber ourselves with debts.

TITHING

*" 'Bring the whole tithe into the
storehouse, so that there may be
food in My house, and test Me now
in this,' says the Lord of hosts, 'if I
will not open for you the windows
of heaven, and pour out for you a
blessing until it overflows.' "*
(Malachi 3:10 NAS).

*G*ive God the first part of your income as a testimony of his ownership. Given as a testimony, God promises to prosper it. God is the only "business manager" who can make 90 percent go farther than 100 percent.

TREASURES

*"Do not lay up for yourselves
treasures upon earth, where
moth and rust destroy, and
where thieves break in and steal.
But lay up for yourselves
treasures in heaven. . .for
where your treasure is,
there will your heart be also"*
(Matthew 6:19-21 NAS).

*T*he treasures of this world are temporary. The treasures of the heart—love, kindness, concern for others—always produce good for those who possess them. Where's the logic for spending a lifetime trying to become rich and ignoring the things that give lasting happiness?

TREASURY

*I*f you are chosen to handle the money for any individual or organization, whether it is for feeding the hungry, supporting missionaries, building a new school or church, or whatever it is for, honesty must be your first priority.

"No accounting was required from the construction superintendents, for they were honest and faithful men"
(2 Kings 12:15 TLB).

TRUST

*I*f we really trust God with everything we have, He will satisfy all our needs as He promised. God gives us small things at first because we are only capable of trusting Him for small things. But as our self-confidence begins to grow and our confidence in Him grows, the more He is able to supply.

"Whoever believes in Him will not be disappointed. . . . for the same Lord is Lord of all, abounding in riches for all who call upon Him"
(Romans 10:11-12 NAS).

TRUSTWORTHINESS

*G*od uses finances to develop our trustworthiness. This principle is important because our lives revolve around the making, spending, investing, or saving of money. God cannot be in control if we allow ourselves to become corrupt in money matters.

"For the Lord knows the way of the righteous, But the way of the wicked will perish"
(Psalm 1:6 NAS).

UNFAIRNESS

*W*e will never know with certainty why God allows problems to come into the lives of some godly people who suffer from unfairness no matter how well they serve others. See the story of Jacob in Genesis 28-30. Though he was treated unfairly for years, everything Jacob touched flourished, and in the end he was the victor.

"Yet what we suffer now is nothing compared to the glory he will give us later" (Romans 8:18 TLB).

UNRIGHTEOUSNESS

*I*f we are not fair and merciful to others, we shouldn't expect to receive fairness and mercy at the hand of our Father.

"Do you not know that the unrighteous shall not inherit the kingdom of God?" (1 Corinthians 6:9 NAS)

USURY

*M*any people use religious contacts as a means to solicit business—approaching others at church and applying pressure because of Christian involvement. Pressure is applied on the basis of church involvement rather the value of what is offered. God warns those caught up in this attitude.

"He who increases his wealth by interest and usury, gathers it for him who is gracious to the poor" (Proverbs 28:8 NAS).

VALUES

Scripture speaks strongly about true values. God's value system is based on spiritual worth. There's a great need to get back to the basics of God's Word. That's true whether we're talking about salvation, service, sanctification, or finances. We have only one purpose for anything—to glorify God.

"Whether then, you eat or drink or whatever you do, do all to the glory of God" (1 Corinthians 10:31 NAS).

VANITY

The extremes of poverty and wealth are both dangerous. Wealth may make us too self-confident and lead us to forget where our wealth came from; poverty may lead us to commit desperate acts that deny our Lord. It's far better to lead a life somewhere between poverty and wealth.

"Give me neither poverty nor riches; feed me with the food that is my portion, lest I be full and deny Thee and say, 'Who is the Lord?'" (Proverbs 30:8-9 NAS)

VOCATION

*Q*uite often putting God first in the area of vocation will necessitate choosing a vocation that has little or no retirement security or ego-building status. But, for a Christian to accept non-Christian vocational goals is to invite future problems. Regardless of income, prestige, or security of a vocation, unless it merges with God's will, unrest will persist.

VOWS

A vow is something made under one set of circumstances that may be broken under another. Few scriptural principles are clearer than that of keeping our vows—literally keeping our word both to God and to others. When you borrow you make a vow to repay.

WAGES

*S*omeone who works for us, whether as a housekeeper, baby-sitter, painter, or corporate executive, deserves an equitable and fair wage for any work that is done.

WEALTH

*A*ccording to our attitudes, wealth can be creative (used to spread God's Word, build hospitals and churches, feed the poor, or take care of orphans), or it can be wasted on frivolous activities and lavish living. It can also be corruptive—used to purchase influence, bribes, illegal transactions, or guns and bombs.

"Honor the Lord
with your wealth,
with the firstfruits
of all your crops"
(Proverbs 3:9 NIV).

WEALTH, INCLUSIVE

*W*ealth is usually thought of in terms of money, land, possessions. But it also includes our creative abilities and our borrowing abilities— the trust others have in us. Thus, wealth becomes an extension of our personalities and character. Wealth is all that God entrusts to us.

"Of course, it is very good if
a man has received wealth
from the Lord, and
the good health to enjoy it. . .
that is indeed a gift from God"
(Ecclesiastes 5:19-20 TLB).

WELFARE

*T*he Bible's stand on welfare is very clear: we are to help those in need. The fact that the government has assumed the function of caring for the poor does not negate our responsibility. Welfare is biblical and necessary.

"You shall freely open your
hand to your brother,
to your needy and
poor in your land"
(Deuteronomy 15:11 NAS).

WIDOWS

"Religion that God our Father accepts as pure and faultless is this: to look after orphans and widows in their distress and to keep oneself from being polluted by the world" (James 1:27 NIV).

*I*t's impossible to read the epistles of James and John without recognizing the requirement to help others in need. We are admonished to meet the needs of the widows and orphans because they are unable to meet their own needs.

WISDOM

"If you count yourself above average in intelligence, as judged by this world's standards, you had better put this all aside and be a fool rather than let it hold you back from the true wisdom from above" (1 Corinthians 3:18 TLB).

*S*urrender control of your finances to God and then accept His wisdom. How can we seek God's wisdom in Christian finances? God says that if we pray anything in His will, believing, it shall be given to us. When we turn our finances over to God, we must also be willing to accept His direction.

WORK

"Whatever you do, do your work heartily, as for the Lord rather than for men. . . .It is the Lord Christ that you serve" (Colossians 3:23-24 NAS).

*S*omehow Christians have been duped into believing that work is a secular activity and therefore one shouldn't expect to feel spiritual about a job. That attitude destroys our greatest area of outreach and witness. Few Christians who view their work as a chore have much of a witness on or off the job.

WORRY

*W*orrying over investments, savings, money, or assets can cause financial bondage and may interfere with our lives. Then worry can spill over into other areas of life. If we are worrying, we are not trusting.

"Don't worry about anything; instead, pray about everything; tell God your needs and don't forget to thank him for his answers" (Philippians 4:6 TLB).

ABOUT THE AUTHOR

Larry Burkett hosts a daily radio program heard on over 1,100 outlets and has written more than fifty books, including best-sellers *Your Finances in Changing Times, Business by the Book, Debt-Free Living, The Coming Economic Earthquake,* and *What Ever Happened to the American Dream.* Larry and his wife Judy currently reside in Gainesville, Georgia. They have four grown children and seven grandchildren.

ABOUT THE EDITOR

Adeline Griffith is Managing Editor of Products and Resources for Christian Financial Concepts in Gainesville, Georgia, where she has been the editor of such books as *The Illuminati, The Coming Economic Earthquake, Investing for the Future, Preparing for Retirement,* and *Damaged but Not Broken,* by Larry Burkett. She also has adapted manuscripts to scripts for several book-on-tape projects for Moody Press and Victor Books.

Christian Financial Concepts Inc.
Teaching | Biblical Principles of Managing Money

Larry Burkett, founder and president of Christian Financial Concepts, earned B.S. degrees in marketing and in finance, and recently an Honorary Doctorate in Economics was conferred by Southwest Baptist University. For several years Larry served as a manager in the space program at Cape Canaveral, Florida. He also has been vice president of an electronics manufacturing firm. Larry's education, business experience, and solid understanding of God's Word enable him to give practical, Bible-based financial counsel to families, churches, and businesses.

Founded in 1976, Christian Financial Concepts, Inc. is a nonprofit, nondenominational ministry dedicated to helping God's people gain a clear understanding of how to manage their money according to scriptural principles. Although practical assistance is provided on many levels, the purpose of CFC is simple *to bring glory to God by freeing His people from financial bondage so they may serve Him to their utmost.*

One major avenue of ministry involves the training of volunteers in budget and debt counseling and linking them with financially troubled families and individuals through a nationwide referral network. CFC also provides financial management seminars and workshops for churches and other groups. (Formats available include audio, video, and live instruction.) A full line of printed and audio-visual materials related to money management is available through CFC's materials department (1-800-722-1976).

Visit CFC's Internet site at http://www.cfcministry.org or write to the address below for further information.

Christian Financial Concepts
PO Box 2458
Gainesville, GA 30503-2458